5-09

YOUR BODY BATTLES AN
EARACHE

WRITTEN BY **VICKI COBB** PHOTOMICROGRAPHS BY **DENNIS KUNKEL**
ILLUSTRATIONS BY **ANDREW N. HARRIS**

M Millbrook Press / Minneapolis

NOTE: The photomicrographs in this book were taken with a scanning electron microscope (SEM). The photos are originally in black and white. Color was added by computer, often to highlight interesting features. The colors used do not show the real colors of the subject. The × followed by a number indicates magnification. For example, ×250 means the object in the picture is 250 times larger than its real size.

For Jillian Davis Cobb—VC

This series is dedicated to my mom, Carmen Kunkel, for the care she gives her children and grandchildren—DK

For Marie, thank you for your love and support—ANH

The author acknowledges the help of the following people but accepts full responsibility for the accuracy of the text: Ali Andalibi, Ph.D., scientist and director, New Technology and Project Development, National Science Foundation; Paul Webster, Ph.D., scientist at the House Ear Institute, Los Angeles, CA; Dr. Stuart T. Nevins, practicing otolaryngologist with Ear, Nose and Throat and Allergy Associates, LLC, White Plains, NY. The author also thanks Mary Slamin and Gail Fell, children's librarians from the Greenburgh, New York Public Library, for assistance with the Further Reading list.

Millbrook Press
A division of Lerner Publishing Group, Inc.
241 First Avenue North
Minneapolis, MN 55401 U.S.A.

Website address: www.lernerbooks.com

Library of Congress Cataloging-in-Publication Data

Cobb, Vicki.
    Your body battles an earache / by Vicki Cobb ; photomicrographs by Dennis Kunkel ; illustrated by Andrew N. Harris.
        p.   cm. — (Body Battles)
    Includes bibliographical references and index.
    ISBN 978-0-8225-6812-4 (lib. bdg. : alk. paper)
    1. Earache in children—Juvenile literature. 2. Earache—Juvenile literature. I. Harris, Andrew, 1977- ill. II. Title.
RF291.5.C45C63 2009
617.8'3—dc22   2008002846

Manufactured in the United States of America
1 2 3 4 5 6 – DP – 14 13 12 11 10 09

Don't you just hate it when you get an earache? Your ear is stuffed. Everything sounds as if your ear is full of cotton. You might even have a fever. And no matter how much you pull on your earlobe or tilt your head one way or the other, the ache just doesn't stop. Your ear has an infection caused by a germ. This book tells the story of how the superheroes of your body will put up an excellent fight to make you well again.

MIDDLE EAR EPITHELIAL CELL

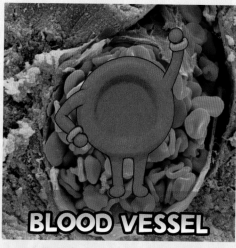

BLOOD VESSEL

NERVE CELL

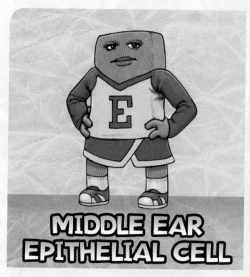

NEUTROPHIL

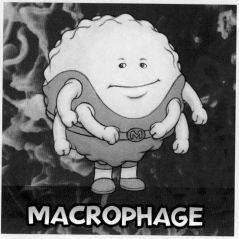

MACROPHAGE

You have many kinds of
cells that do different jobs
in your body.

Nerve cells send messages to and from the brain and spinal cord to all parts of the body. Muscle cells allow you to move. Bone cells keep bone hard and healthy. Red blood cells carry oxygen to all parts of the body. Among other things, skin cells prevent germs from entering your body.

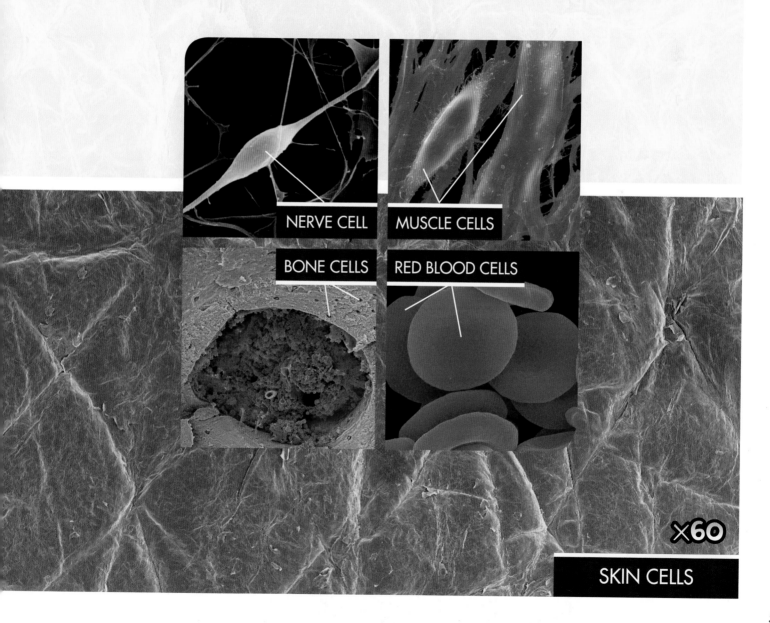

NERVE CELL

MUSCLE CELLS

BONE CELLS

RED BLOOD CELLS

X60

SKIN CELLS

An earache comes from germs attacking the cells in your ears. To understand how that happens, you have to understand how the ear is built. The part you think of as your ear, the part that is attached to the outside of your head, is a funnel to catch sound. Scientists call it the pinna. Sound travels from your pinna into a tube called a canal. A doctor can see the end of the canal using a lighted magnifying instrument called an otoscope.

You can use your hands to make your pinnas into super ears. Cup your hands behind your pinnas. Are some sounds now louder? Do you hear some sounds you didn't notice before? Cup your hands in front of each ear on either side of your head, facing backward. Can you hear some sounds behind you that you didn't notice before?

The canal is sealed off with a thin piece of skin stretched over the opening. It is so much like the material stretched over a drum that it is called the eardrum.

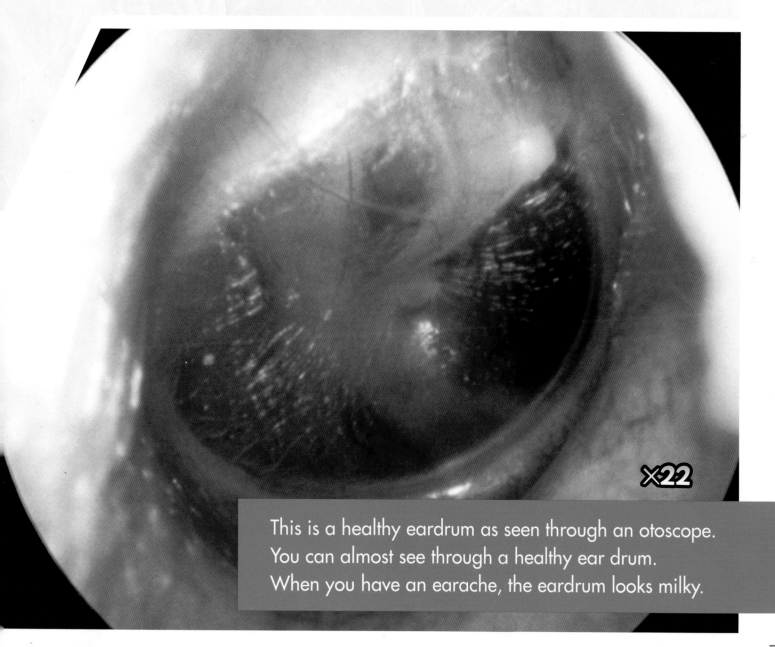

×22

This is a healthy eardrum as seen through an otoscope.
You can almost see through a healthy ear drum.
When you have an earache, the eardrum looks milky.

When sound hits your eardrum, it makes the eardrum move back and forth very quickly. These back and forth movements are called vibrations.

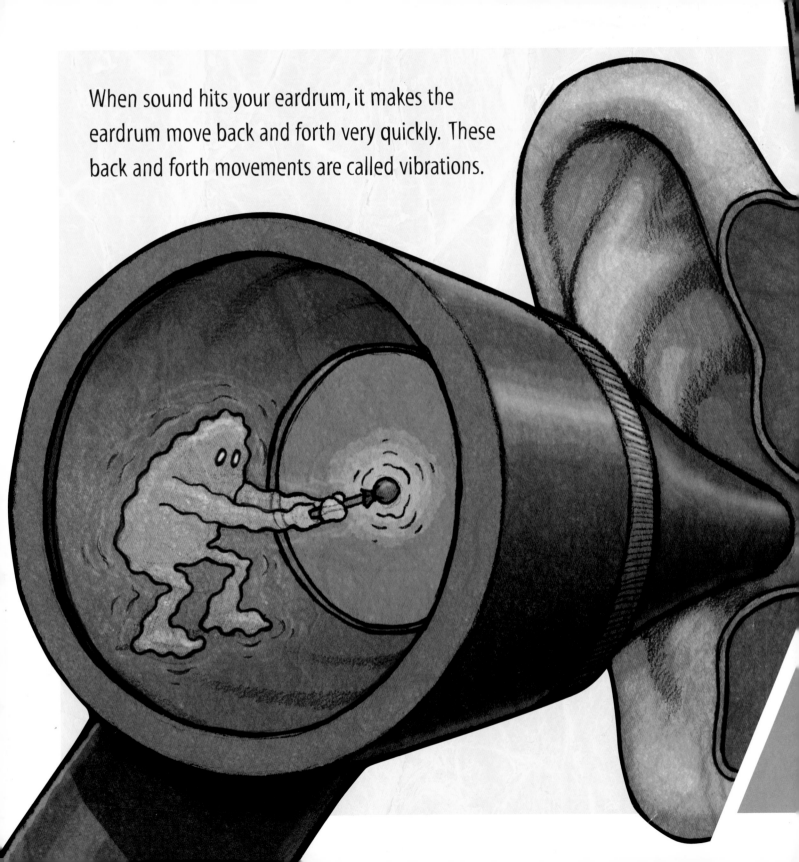

You can see how the eardrum vibrates. Make a drum by stretching some plastic wrap tightly over a bowl. Sprinkle about a teaspoon of sugar all over the stretched plastic. Then make some noise by banging a pot with a spoon over your "drum." The sound vibrations make the plastic wrap vibrate, and this makes the sugar dance.

Behind your eardrum is a space
about the size of a pea. This space is known as the middle ear.
Three very tiny bones, the smallest bones in your body, make a chain
across the space. One end bone is attached to the eardrum.
The middle bone acts like a hinge. The bone at the other end
is attached to a snail-shaped structure called the cochlea.

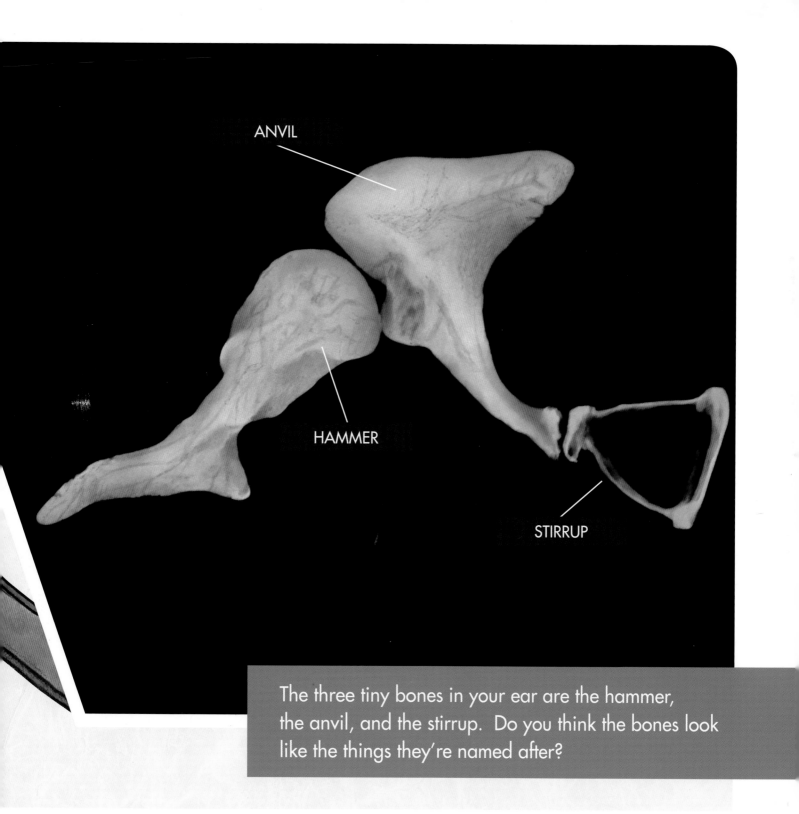

ANVIL

HAMMER

STIRRUP

The three tiny bones in your ear are the hammer, the anvil, and the stirrup. Do you think the bones look like the things they're named after?

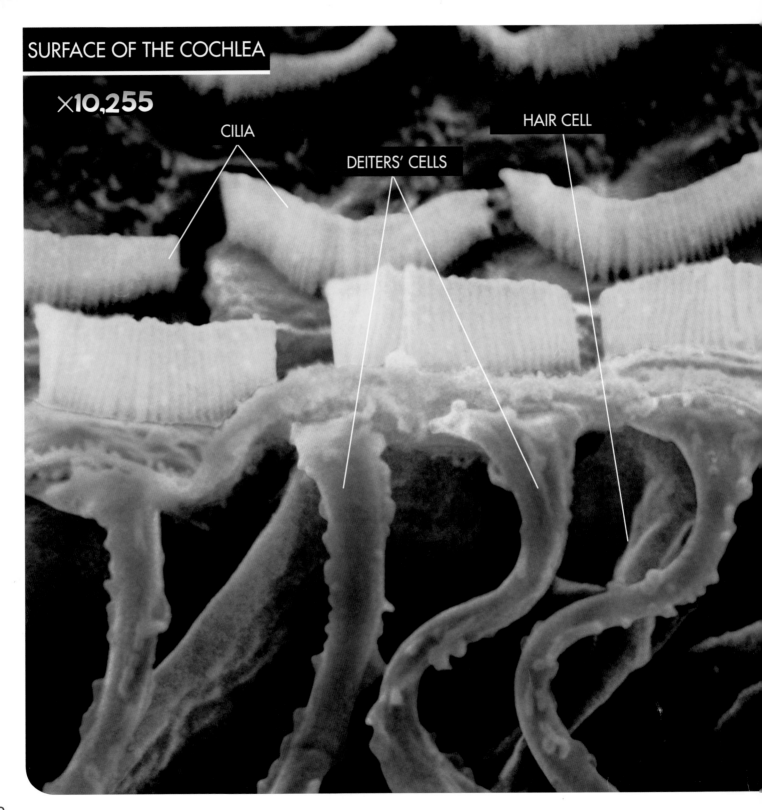

SURFACE OF THE COCHLEA

×10,255

CILIA

DEITERS' CELLS

HAIR CELL

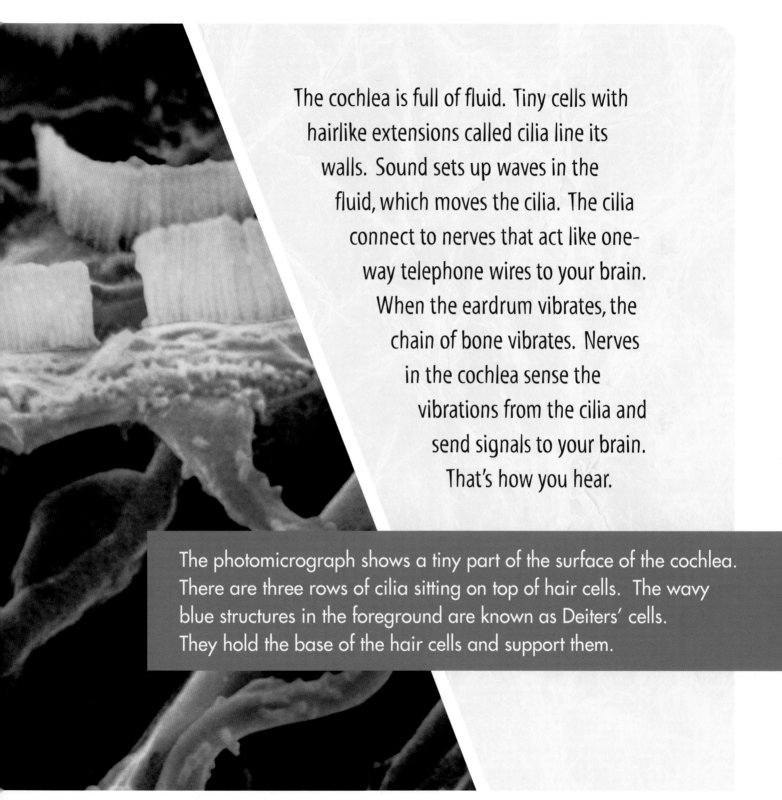

The cochlea is full of fluid. Tiny cells with hairlike extensions called cilia line its walls. Sound sets up waves in the fluid, which moves the cilia. The cilia connect to nerves that act like one-way telephone wires to your brain. When the eardrum vibrates, the chain of bone vibrates. Nerves in the cochlea sense the vibrations from the cilia and send signals to your brain. That's how you hear.

The photomicrograph shows a tiny part of the surface of the cochlea. There are three rows of cilia sitting on top of hair cells. The wavy blue structures in the foreground are known as Deiters' cells. They hold the base of the hair cells and support them.

When you go up in an elevator or an airplane, slightly less air presses on your eardrum. The air in your middle ear then presses outward on your eardrum, and your ear feels "stuffed." If you yawn, some air comes out your eustachian tube and your ear feels normal again.

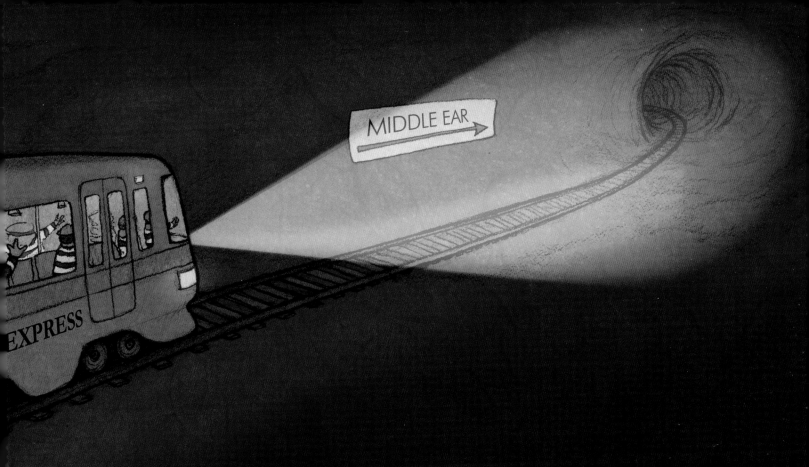

A tube connects your middle ear to the back of your throat. It's called the eustachian tube. The eustachian tube makes sure that the middle ear is always full of air. Your earache happens in this tiny middle space, known as the middle ear. Germs can travel from your throat through the eustachian tube into your middle ear.

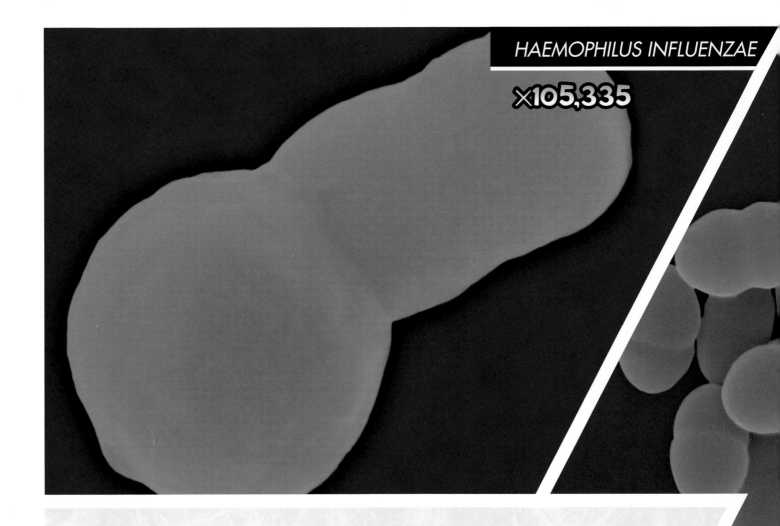

There are three main kinds of bacteria, pictured here, that can cause an earache. *Haemophilus influenzae (above)* got its name because people once thought it caused flu. It doesn't, but it does cause infections in the eye as well as the ear. The green bacteria to the right causes pneumonia as well as ear infections. And the purple bacteria can also cause heavy coughing and make you lose your voice.

STREPTOCOCCUS PNEUMONIAE

×42,500

Bacteria have different shapes. Some are round, and some are like rods. They need warm, moist places to grow and reproduce themselves. Your middle ear space can be a home for them.

MORAXELLA CATARRHALIS

×34,000

These three types of bacteria cause most earaches in children.

The bacteria that can cause an earache often live in the back of your throat where they don't make you sick. But if they manage to get in your middle ear, they change and become an enemy. Scientists are trying to find out why that happens.

Once the bacteria get to the middle ear, they can attach themselves to the surface of the cells lining your middle ear. They may even form a kind of slimy coating on your skin cells. It's something like the coating you feel on your teeth when you wake up in the morning.

Your middle ear skin cells find this coating very irritating. They begin to do things to get rid of the enemy.

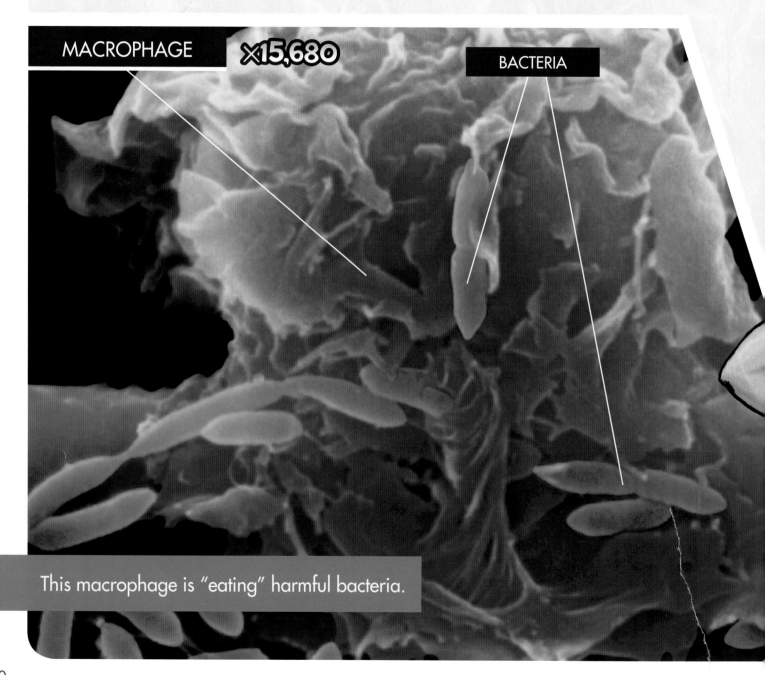

MACROPHAGE

X15,680

BACTERIA

This macrophage is "eating" harmful bacteria.

Some cells of the middle ear can produce a weapon to make holes in bacteria, which kills them. Some of your blood cells also get involved. White blood cells known as macrophages and neutrophils, can "eat" the bacteria by wrapping around them, pulling them inside, and dissolving them.

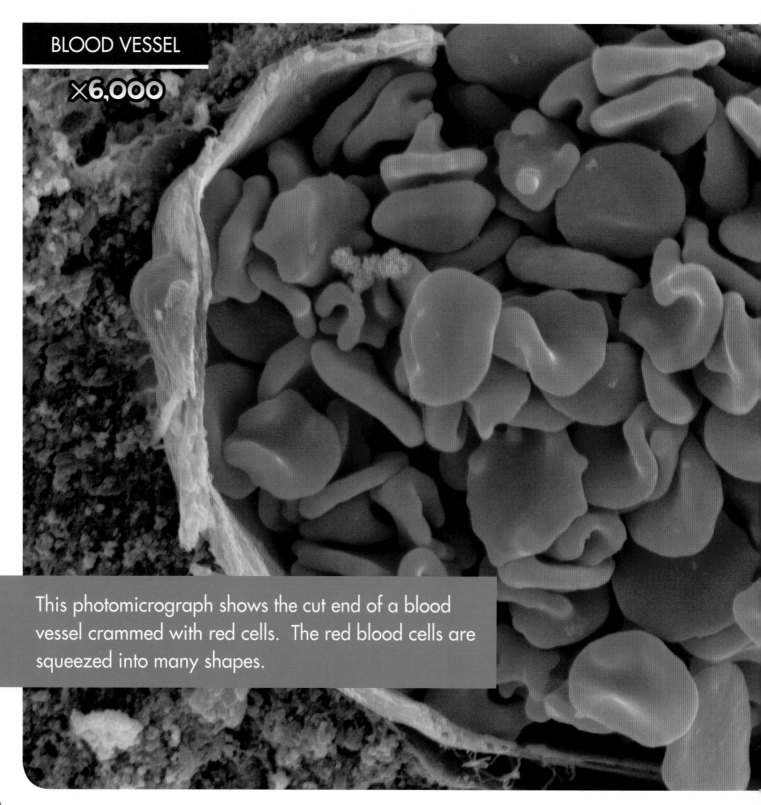

This photomicrograph shows the cut end of a blood vessel crammed with red cells. The red blood cells are squeezed into many shapes.

Your attacked cells also give off a kind of juice that sends a message to the nearby tubes carrying blood, called blood vessels. The message tells the blood vessels to open wider so that they can carry lots more blood to your middle ear. More blood brings more food, oxygen, and white blood cells to the battle. It also brings a lot more fluid. Clear fluid seeps through your cells into the space in your middle ear. It's as if your body is trying to wash away the bacteria. The fluid also protects the eardrum from collapsing.

23

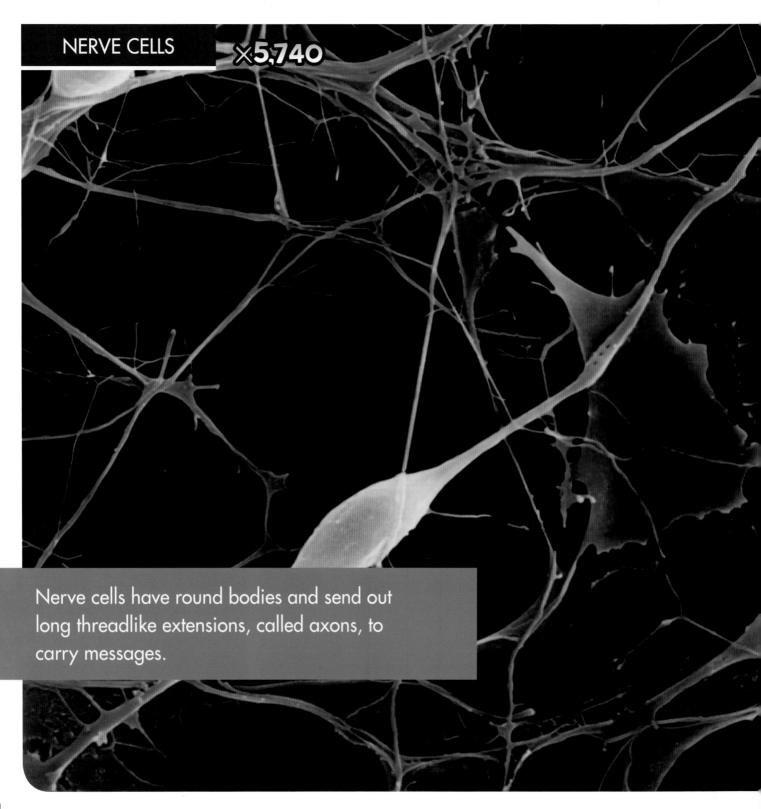

Nerve cells have round bodies and send out long threadlike extensions, called axons, to carry messages.

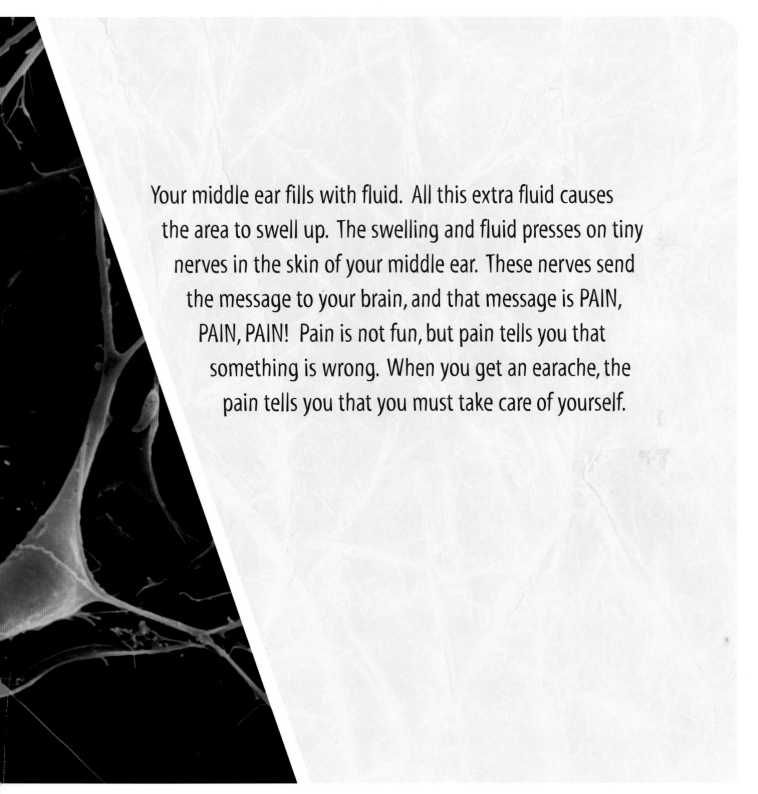

Your middle ear fills with fluid. All this extra fluid causes the area to swell up. The swelling and fluid presses on tiny nerves in the skin of your middle ear. These nerves send the message to your brain, and that message is PAIN, PAIN, PAIN! Pain is not fun, but pain tells you that something is wrong. When you get an earache, the pain tells you that you must take care of yourself.

For many years, doctors would almost always prescribe an antibiotic to
kill the bacteria in an aching ear. But they found that if this medicine
was used too often, the bacteria changed so that the antibiotic
was no longer able to kill them. Too much medicine is not a good
thing. Besides, often the body is pretty good at killing the bacteria
without help.

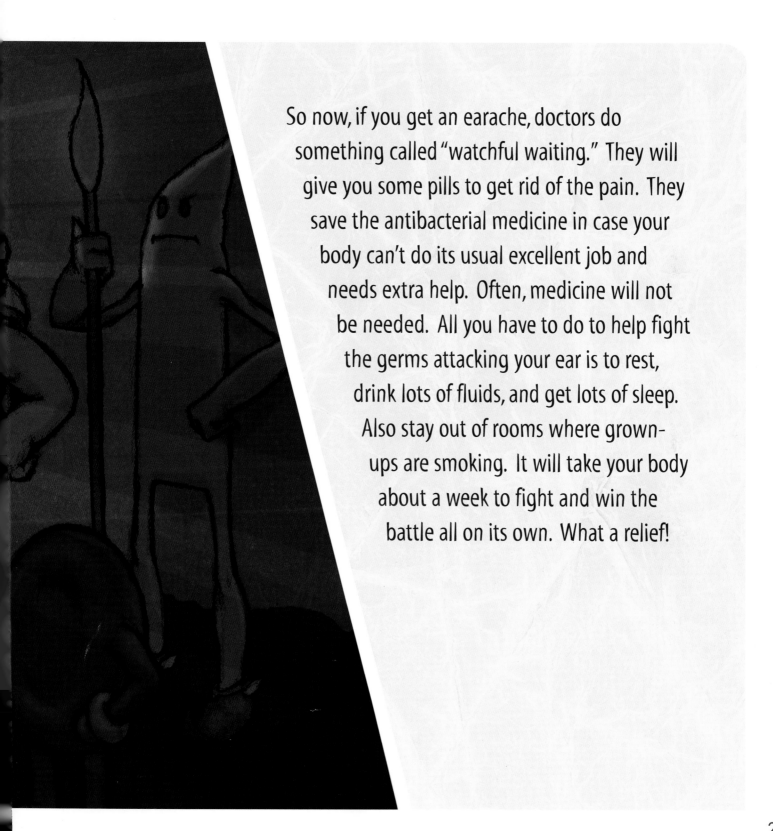

So now, if you get an earache, doctors do something called "watchful waiting." They will give you some pills to get rid of the pain. They save the antibacterial medicine in case your body can't do its usual excellent job and needs extra help. Often, medicine will not be needed. All you have to do to help fight the germs attacking your ear is to rest, drink lots of fluids, and get lots of sleep. Also stay out of rooms where grown-ups are smoking. It will take your body about a week to fight and win the battle all on its own. What a relief!

GLOSSARY

antibiotic: medicine that kills infection-causing bacteria (germs)

anvil: the middle of a chain of three tiny bones in the middle ear that transmit sound vibrations from the eardrum to the cochlea

bacteria: single-celled microorganisms that can live independently or on other living things. Some bacteria cause infections.

blood vessels: tubes that carry blood. Veins carry blood back to the heart. Arteries carry blood from the heart to the rest of the body. Capillaries connect arteries and veins.

cells: the smallest units of all living things considered to be alive. The smallest living things have only one cell. Human beings are multicelled.

cochlea: a spiral, snail-shaped structure in the inner ear containing nerves to sense sound vibrations and send them to the brain

eardrum: a thin membrane that stretches across the end of the ear canal. It vibrates when sound in the air strikes it. This vibration is then transmitted to three tiny bones that attach to the other side of the eardrum in the middle ear.

epithelial cells: cells that are found lining all the surfaces of the body, inside and out

eustachian tube: a tiny tube that connects the middle ear with the back of the throat. It equalizes air pressure on the eardrum.

hammer: the tiny bone attached to the inside of the eardrum. The hammer starts the chain of three little bones that conduct sound vibrations from the eardrum to the cochlea.

macrophage: a white blood cell that cleans up sick and infected areas by "eating" germs and dead cells

microscope: a powerful magnifier that allows us to look at cells. There are two main kinds of microscopes:

An **optical microscope** uses light and can magnify up to 1,500 times the actual size.

An **electron microscope** uses electrons and can magnify even smaller structures. The two types of electron microscopes are scanning (SEM), which can magnify up to 500,000 times, and transmission (TEM), which can magnify up to a million times.

middle ear: the space between the eardrum and the cochlea containing a chain of three tiny bones. The bones conduct sound vibrations from the eardrum to the sense organ that will transmit to the brain. Most common ear infections occur in the middle ear.

neutrophils: a type of white blood cell that cleans up infections, similar to macrophages

otoscope: an instrument used by doctors to examine the eardrum and inside of the ear canal. It consists of a magnifying lens and a flashlight.

pinna: the skin and cartilage on the side of your head that you think of as your ear. Its job is to collect sound waves and focus them as they move down your ear canal.

red blood cells: the cells in the blood responsible for carrying oxygen to all parts of the body. Their red color comes from iron in each cell.

stirrup: the third bone in a chain of three that connects the eardrum to the cochlea. The stirrup is attached to the cochlea.

vibrations: rapid back and forth motion. Sound is the vibrations of molecules.

white blood cells: colorless cells floating in the blood. They are important to the immune system and for fighting disease.

FURTHER READING

Balkwill, Fran. *Cell Wars*. Minneapolis: Millbrook Press, 1993.

Ballard, Carol. *Ears: Injury, Illness and Health*. Portsmouth, NH: Heinemann, 2003.

Johnson, Rebecca L. *Daring Cell Defenders*. Minneapolis: Millbrook Press, 2008.

Silverstein, Alvin, Virginia Silverstein, and Laura Silverstein Nunn. *Earaches*. Danbury, CT: Franklin Watts, 2002.

Simon, Seymour. *Eyes and Ears*. New York: HarperCollins, 2003.

WEBSITES

KidsHealth

http://www.kidshealth.org/kid/body/ear_noSW.html
A kid-friendly site called "Let's Hear It for the Ear!" offers a general explanation of how the ear works. Another site from the same source clearly explains earaches: http://www.kidshealth.org/kid/ill_injure/sick/ear_infection.html.

Neuroscience for Kids

http://faculty.washington.edu/chudler/bigear.html
This site segment uses experiments to explain how the ear functions.

INDEX